CRITTERS OF MICHIGAN POCKET GUIDE

Produced in cooperation with Wildlife Forever

by Ann E. McCarthy, Director of Education

Adventure Publications, Inc.
Cambridge, Minnesota

Dedication

To my parents with great appreciation and affection.

– Ann E. McCa

Thanks, also, to K.L. Cool, Director, Michigan Department of Na Resources, for his thoughtful dedication to conserving Michig wildlife.

Research and Editorial Assistance, David A. Frederick

Technical Editor, Ray Rustem, Natural Heritage Unit, Divisio Wildlife, Michigan Department of Natural Resources

This publication was funded in part by the Nadalynn Conway Tru

Cover, interior design and illustrations: Jonathan Norberg

Photo Credits: **Dominique Braud**: 64, 68 (perch) **Mary Clay/DPA**: 3C **Brian Collins**: 106 (female) **Sharon Cummings/DPA**: 18, 94 (male), **E.R. Degginger/DPA**: 46, 70 **Dan Dempster/DPA**: 82 (female) **Du Edmondson**: 22, 28, 34 (winter), 68 (soar), 86 (both), 108 (male) **Gerlach/DPA**: 48 **Richard Haug**: 40 **Adam Jones/DPA**: 62 (female) (male) **Rolf Kopfle/DPA**: 88 **Bill Lea/DPA**: 14 **Doug Locke/DPA**: 56 (female) **Bill Marchel**: 32, 60 (both) **Maslowski Productions**: 20 (summer), 36, 38, 44, 54 (winter), 58, 84, 90, 96 (male), 104, (female) **Gary Meszaros/DPA**: 42 **John Mielcarek/DPA**: 24, 52 **Moody/DPA**: 12, 26, 62 (male), 78, 92 **Alan Nelson/DPA**: 10, 16, 5C **Stan Osolinski/DPA**: 54 (summer) **Rod Planck/DPA**: 98 **Polking/DPA**: 80 **Carl R. Sams II/DPA**: 72, 96 (female) **Ge Stewart/DPA**: 100 **Stan Tekiela**: 106 (male) **Brian Wheeler**: 76 (bc DPA=Dembinsky Photo Associates

ABOUT WILDLIFE FOREVER

Wildlife Forever is a nonprofit conservation organization dedicated to conserving America's wildlife heritage through education, preservation of habitat and management of fish and wildlife. Working at the grassroots level, Wildlife Forever has completed conservation projects in all 50 states. Wildlife Forever's innovative outreach programs include the Wildlife Forever State-Fish Art Project and the Theodore Roosevelt Conservation Partnership.

Cry of the Wild

The "cry of the wild" can still be heard across this great land. I have heard the bugle of an elk amid the foothills of the western plains…the shrill of a bald eagle along the banks of the mighty Mississippi…the roar of a brown bear on windswept tundra…the thunder of migrating waterfowl on coastal shores…the gobble of a wild turkey among eastern hardwoods and the haunting cry of a sandhill crane in the wetlands of the Central Flyway. America is truly blessed—a land rich in natural resources. This legacy must be preserved.

I hope this book will provide you with an insight to the many wonders of the natural world and serve as a stepping-stone to the great outdoors.

Yours for wildlife…forever,

Douglas H. Grann
President & CEO, Wildlife Forever

To learn more contact us at 763-253-0222, 2700 Freeway Blvd., Ste. 1000, Brooklyn Center, MN 55430 or check out our website at www.wildlifeforever.org.

TABLE OF CONTENTS

irds

FOREWORD
by Director Keith Creagh,
Michigan Department of Natural Resources

Michigan's great outdoors feed the imagination. Close your eyes for a moment and conjure up the sights and sounds of Michigan's wild places—a raptor soaring through a clear blue sky; the bugle of a bull elk in a fall forest; the distant gobble of a wild turkey in the morning fog; the howl of a wolf breaking up the steady crackle of an evening campfire; the call of a loon across a still lake.

This is the wildlife of Michigan. You can share these experiences and many others simply by spending time outdoors and learning the habits of these magnificent creatures. You may choose to hunt game species or to observe the natural world from a distance. Either way, Michigan's wildlife is among the finest in the world.

The *Critters of Michigan Pocket Guide* is a fun way to begin exploring our state's natural resources. The guide offers information on simple identifying characteristics, unique behavior, and diverse habitats that provide homes for Michigan's birds and mammals. Although it is not a complete list, it is a great start. You can discover interesting facts and countless viewing opportunities for wildlife around the state by visiting the DNR's website www.michigan.gov/dnr.

While you continue to learn about Michigan's world-class natural resources, our department will continue its mission to protect and manage those resources for current and future generations. Now that sounds like a great partnership!

Keith Creagh
Director, Michigan Department of Natural Resources
530 W. Allegan St., P.O. Box 30028
Lansing, MI 48909

FACTS
About Michigan

...ichigan. The name comes from the Chippewa Indian ...ord "meicigama" which means "great water." With more ...an 38,575 square miles of Great Lakes water area, ...ichigan is truly the "Great Lakes State." Michigan is the ...ly state that touches four out of the five Great Lakes: Lake ...uperior, Lake Michigan, Lake Huron and Lake Erie. In fact, ...and anywhere in Michigan and you are within 85 miles of ...ne of these Great Lakes. Because it is adjacent to these ...rge bodies of water and because it has 11,000 inland ...kes and 36,000 miles of streams, Michigan has the most ...eshwater shoreline in the world.

...esides the abundance of water, Michigan's Upper and ...ower Peninsulas are comprised of a large variety of land ...orms—about 38,575 square miles of land. The land ranges ...om sand dunes to rolling hills to level plains to swamps ...nd the rugged Porcupine Mountains.

...ll this water and varied topography are good for wildlife and ...ildlife viewing. From Isle Royale National Park, home to ...ne of the largest moose herds remaining in the U. S., to the ...eney National Wildlife Refuge and its 250 species of birds ...nd 50 species of mammals, Michigan is a great place for ...ildlife and for people who appreciate the great outdoors.

State Bird: American Robin	**State Flower:** Apple Blossom	**State Wildflower:** Dwarf Lake Iris
State Tree: White Pine	**State Fish:** Brook Trout	**State Game Mammal:** White-tailed Deer
State Stone: Petoskey Stone	**State Gem:** Chlorastrolite	**State Reptile:** Painted Turtle

How to Use This Guide

While this book is not intended as a field guide (we don'
want anyone getting too close to a bear trying to identify i
species!), it is intended to be a great reference for informa
tion on some of the fascinating animals that we loosely ca
the "critters" of Michigan. We think that the more informa
tion people have about wildlife and their needs, the more w
can do to conserve this wonderful part of our natural worlc

Notes About Icons

In the mammal section, the track
one foot is included near the bottor
right of the page. The size, from top t
bottom is included beside it. Whe
appropriate, the front and hind print ar
included with the front placed at the to
of the oval, and the hind at the bottom. Note that for som
animals such as the cottontail, you will find that in a set o
tracks, the hind print actually appears ahead of the fron
This will be apparent in the layout of the tracks as shown i
the right margin. While the sizes of the individual tracks ar
relative to each other, the pattern of tracks is not. We woul
have needed a very large page to accomodate the moos
tracks compared to the chipmunk!

The animal/person silhouette on the bc
tom left of the mammal pages is to sho
the relative size of the animal compare
to an averaged-sized adult. Sometime
it's easier to judge comparisons tha
actual measurements.

nocturnal (active at night)

diurnal (active during day)

crepuscular (most active at dawn and dusk)

hibernator/deep sleeper (dormant during winter)

The yellow symbols depicting the sun, moon or the sun on the horizon indicate whether the animal is nocturnal, diurnal or crepuscular. While you may see these animals at other times, they are most active during the periods shown. The yellow Zzzs indicate whether or not the animal hibernates. Some critters are true hibernators, which means their body processes slow down a great deal and they require very little energy to survive the winter. Other critters are deep sleepers, and their body processes slow down only a little and they require greater amounts of energy to survive the winter.

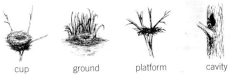

| cup | ground | platform | cavity |

On the bird pages, the nest type is shown at the bottom right. This indicates whether the bird builds a ground nest, a cup-type nest, a platform nest or a cavity nest.

On the Lifelist on page 110, place a check by each mammal or bird you've seen, whether in your backyard or at the zoo.

DID YOU KNOW...? The American badger uses its digging ability to dig itself out of trouble. It can dig at a faster rate than a person can dig with a shovel. While digging, the badger sends dirt flying 4-5' into the air. Although the badger has very short legs and walks in a pigeon-toed fashion (toes pointed in), it can still reach speeds of 10-15 mph.

BADGER, AMERICAN
Taxidea taxus

Size: body 20-35" long; tail 4-6" long: stands 9" high at shoulder; weighs 13-30 lbs.

Habitat: prairies and farmland

Range: across the state but becoming rare in far north

Food: snakes, chipmunks, woodchucks, rabbits, turtle eggs, ground-nesting birds' eggs; may burrow into dens of some of these prey

Mating: during August to September resulting in gestation of about 7 months until birth of young

Den: grass-lined; located 2-6' underground

Young: 3-7 young born blind; eyes open at 4-6 weeks; nurse for 4-6 weeks; later learn to hunt; independent at 10-12 weeks

Predators: wolverine, lynx, coyote, wolf, bobcat, cougar and bear

Tracks: 5 toes and a soft, medium-sized pad, with long claw imprints

Description: Usually seen along roadsides or railways, the badger has a wide, flattened body with short fur that is silver-gray to yellowish gray. It also has a broad, wedge-shaped head with a white stripe that runs from the nose, over the head, and down the back. It has short powerful legs with 2" claws and spends most of the time underground. Mostly active at night.

2¼"

DID YOU KNOW...? The bat is the only mammal capable of flight. It uses echolocation (sound waves) to detect and catch insects. It is capable of catching 600 moths in one hour and thousands of mosquitoes in a single night. Each fall, as temperatures begin to drop and the numbers of insects decline, they migrate to favorite hibernation sites and return to breeding sites in late spring.

BAT, LITTLE BROWN
Myotis lucifugus

Size: 3-4½" in length with a 1½" forearm; males and females each weigh ¼ -⅓ of an ounce with a wingspan of 8-9"

Habitat: often in wooded areas near water and large insect populations

Range: common across state in rural, urban and suburban areas alike

Food: insects including moths, mosquitoes, beetles and crickets

Mating: prior to hibernation each fall resulting in gestation of 60 days until birth of young (after delayed implantation of 7 months)

Nest Site: colonize and roost in groups in attics and other buildings, tree cavities and caves

Young: one pup is born, commonly in maternity colonies of 300-600 females; dark brown in color, they weigh 30% of adult and nurse for approximately 4 weeks; able to fly at 3 weeks

Predators: owls, hawks, snakes, raccoons, domestic cats

Tracks: none

Description: Bats have a coat of silky hair, cinnamon-buff to dark brown in color, with pale gray undersides and hand-like wings. They are most active at dawn and dusk, skimming the water's surface where they catch insects at a rate of one every eight seconds.

no tracks

DID YOU KNOW...? The black bear is an excellent climber. It can run at speeds of 25 mph. It loves honey and will rip open a beehive to obtain it. Its thick coat protects it from bee stings. While not a true hibernator, the black bear spends up to three months in its den during the winter, living off its stored body fat.

crepuscular **Z**zz *deep sleeper*

BEAR, BLACK
Ursus americanus

Size: body 4½-5' long; stands 2-3' high at shoulder; weighs 250-300 lbs.

Habitat: forests, swamps, wooded parklands and remote areas with dense cover; sometimes seen near edges of suburban areas

Range: found in the Upper Peninsula and in northern parts of Lower Peninsula

Food: nuts, roots, berries, insects, mice and other small mammals, fish and garbage

Mating: during June to July resulting in gestation of about 7-8 months until birth of young

Den: located in brush piles, hollow logs, under fallen trees or beneath uprooted trees

Young: cubs, usually twins, born blind and hairless with pinkish skin; 8" long; 8 oz; eyes open at 40 days; cubs nurse and remain in den until spring; independent at 18 months

Predators: wolves may attack wintering bears, cougar may attack sickly or old bears

Tracks: note big toe on outside of foot

Description: Fur is usually black, but it can be light brown or reddish brown. Most active at dawn and dusk, it marks trees with scent and fur. Signs may include torn-apart logs and hornet nests where bears have been.

4½"

DID YOU KNOW...? A beaver can chew down as many as hundreds of trees each year. One family of beaver may consume as much as a ton (2,000 lbs.) of bark in a single winter. To maintain water level, beavers may build dams up to 100 yards long. The beaver is specially adapted to life underwater with waterproof fur, webbed feet, goggle-like eyelids and nose and ear flaps. It's able to hold its breath for 15 minutes.

(*nocturnal*   *crepuscular*

BEAVER, AMERICAN
Castor canadensis

Size: body 27-35" long; tail 15" long, 7" wide; weighs 28-75 lbs.

Habitat: near fresh water streams, rivers or lakes bordered by trees

Range: across the state

Food: in spring and summer, leaves, buds, twigs, fruit, ferns, stems and roots of aquatic plants; in fall and winter, cuttings from trees stored underwater

Mating: during November to March resulting in gestation of 100-110 days until birth of young

Den: lodge; dome-shaped structure, 2-10' tall, 12-14' wide, with underwater entrance;

Young: 3-5 kits born with thick dark fur; 1 lb. each; able to swim soon after birth; nurse for 8-10 weeks; fully independent at 2 years

Predators: wolverine, lynx, coyote, wolf, bobcat, cougar and bear

Tracks: often erased by tail as it drags behind

Description: The beaver is a large rodent with prominent orange teeth, and a large, flat, paddle-shaped tail. It is most active at night, late afternoon and daybreak. Look for tree cuttings near the shoreline and mud mounds marked with scent. Listen for tail slaps on the water.

6"

DID YOU KNOW...? Found only in North America, and the most common wildcat here, the bobcat is named for its stubby, "bobbed" tail. It can leap 7-10' in a single bound. An excellent climber, it uses trees for resting, observation and protection. It can travel 3-7 miles for a hunt and stores uneaten food under vegetation. Signs may include scratch marks on trees and shredded bark nearby.

(nocturnal   crepuscular

BOBCAT
Lynx rufus

Size: body 26-36" long; tail 4-7" long; stands 20-30" high at shoulder; weighs 15-40 lbs.

Habitat: remote timbered marshlands and dense forests

Range: mostly in Upper Peninsula but also in northern third of Lower Peninsula in forested areas

Food: rabbits, mice, squirrels, mink, muskrat, skunk, fox, porcupine, birds, bats, snakes, frogs and the remains of dead animals (carrion)

Mating: during January to February resulting in gestation of 50-70 days until birth of young

Den: located in hollow logs, on rocky ledges and in caves and brush piles

Young: 2-3 kittens born blind; 10" long; 12 oz. each; eyes open a few days after birth; kittens nurse for 8 weeks; begin to eat meat at 4 weeks; fully independent at 5 months

Predators: adults attacked by cougars, young by foxes and horned owls

Tracks: large, cat-like with 4 toes and a larger rear pad

Description: The bobcat has a yellowish gray coat with reddish brown streaks and a sprinkling of black and a soft beige underside. It is mostly gray during winter months.

2"

DID YOU KNOW...? The Eastern chipmunk is able to run 15 feet per second. It uses its outsized cheek pouches to store and carry food. Frost causes it to head for its den, where it spends a few weeks to several months in a deep sleep. It wakes now and then to eat stored food.

CHIPMUNK, EASTERN
Tamias striatus

Size: body 3-5" long; tail 3-4" long; 2½-4½ oz.

Habitat: wooded and brushy areas with loose soil

Range: across the state

Food: nuts, buds, berries, seeds, mice and insects

Mating: twice each year during February to April and June to July resulting in gestation of 31 days until birth of young

Den: part of burrow with several chambers including a pantry, bathroom and bedroom; entrance is 1½" across; often found under rock piles, brush piles and tangled roots

Young: 1-8 young born blind and hairless; 0.1 oz.; 2 litters per year, fuzzy coat appears at 2 weeks; eyes open at 4 weeks; fully independent at 8 weeks

Predators: coyotes, bobcats, foxes, hawks, owls, weasels snakes and domestic cats

Tracks: difficult to find because of small size; front prints show 4 toes, hind prints show 5

Description: Commonly seen in rural and suburban areas, the Eastern chipmunk is reddish brown with 5 dark stripes alternating with gray; lighter underparts. Active throughout the day, it leaves a trail of chewed nutshells. Its call is a quick "chip-chip-chip."

⅝"

1"

DID YOU KNOW...? Burrows provide winter cover for the cottontail. A group of burrows is called a "warren." Although the cottontail has great eyesight and speed, as well as protective coloring, it is the most preyed-upon animal in North America, having many predators.

COTTONTAIL, EASTERN
Sylvilagus floridanus

Size: body 14-18" long; tail 2" long; weighs 2-4 lbs.

Habitat: pastures, open woodlands, near wetlands

Range: primarily southern Lower and northern Lower Peninsula

Food: in summer alfalfa, dandelion, clover, berries, garden crops; in winter, tree bark, twigs, shrubs; eats own scat for added food value

Mating: during January to September resulting in gestation of 28 days until birth of young

Nest Site: 5" deep depression (burrow) lined with plant material and fur; usually found in meadows or at the base of trees

Young: 4-7 kittens born hairless and blind; 4" long; 1 oz. each; 3-4 litters per year; eyes open at 1 week; young nurse for 4 weeks; fully independent at 5 weeks

Predators: almost every flesh-eating animal including hawks, eagles, falcons, owls, coyotes, foxes, wolves and wolverines

Tracks: toe pads don't show clearly, because of thick fur covering the feet

Description: Found in brushy rural and suburban areas, his grayish brown rabbit has rusty colored fur behind its ears. It has a fluffy, cottony white tail and is most active t night but is often seen feeding at sunrise and sunset.

1"

3½"

DID YOU KNOW...? Known as "the trickster" in certain Native American folklore because of its clever ways, the coyote is unique to North America. It's capable of running at speeds of more than 30 mph. Its distinct howl, coupled with short, high-pitched yelps, can be heard as far away as three miles.

 diurnal *crepuscular*

COYOTE
Canis latrans

Size: body 32-40" long; tail 12-15" long; stands 15-20" high at shoulder; weighs 18-30 lbs.

Habitat: forests, farmland and parkland

Range: throughout Michigan

Food: mice, squirrels, rabbits and other small mammals, birds, frogs, snakes, fish, an occasional deer, and the remains of dead animals (carrion); stores uneaten food under leaves and soil

Mating: during January to April resulting in gestation of 58-63 days until birth

Den: found in roots of old trees, on hillsides, in gravel pits, in wooded thickets, under hollow logs, or in a bank along the water's edge

Young: 5-10 pups born blind and grayish; 8 oz. each; eyes open at 8-14 days; pups nurse for several weeks; later both adults feed pups regurgitated food; independent at 6-9 months

Predators: wolves, golden eagles, cougars and bears

Tracks: look like medium-sized dog tracks with 4 toes and a rear pad

Description: The coyote has a light brown to gray coat with reddish sides and an off-white underside and a black-tipped bushy tail. It is most active in early morning and evening.

2½"

DID YOU KNOW...? The white-tailed deer is the Michigan State Game Mammal. When alarmed, the white-tailed deer raises its tail resembling a white flag. It can run up to 35-40 mph. Prior to breeding, males spar with sapling trees, creating "rub" marks to make other males aware of their presence.

crepuscular

DEER, WHITE-TAILED
Odocoileus virginianus

Size: body 4-6' long; tail 6-13" long; stands 2-3' high at shoulder; males weigh 100-300 lbs., females weigh 85-130 lbs.

Habitat: woodlands, swamps and grasslands

Range: throughout state

Food: in summer, mushrooms, wildflowers and crops; in winter, acorns and bark from willow, oak, birch and maple trees

Mating: during October to January resulting in 7 months gestation until birth of young; males make "scrapes," which are patches of muddy ground where they urinate to attract females

Bedding Site: shallow depressions in hidden, grassy areas; beds down in a different spot each night

Young: 1 or 2 fawns born with white spots for camouflage; spots remain for 3-4 months; 8 lbs. each; fawns nurse for several months; males independent at 1 year, females at 2 years

Predators: wolves, coyotes, bears, bobcats and cougars

Tracks: narrow, heart-shaped with split hoof

Description: Commonly seen in rural and suburban areas, the deer have a reddish brown coat in summer, grayish brown in winter. In spring, males grow forward-facing antlers that are shed in winter.

3"

DID YOU KNOW...? Before European settlers arrived in North America, there were approximately 10 million elk. By the early 1900s, however, the elk population had dropped significantly. Today, thanks to conservation efforts, the elk population has grown to nearly 1 million.

crepuscular

ELK
Cervus elaphus

Size: body 5-8' long; tail 3-8" long; stands 2-5' at shoulder; weighs 500-1,000 lbs.

Habitat: open woodlands

Range: northeastern quarter of the Lower Peninsula

Food: grass, buds, herbs and mushrooms in summer; twigs, bark and grass beneath snow in winter

Mating: during September to October resulting in gestation of 8 months from pregnancy until birth of young

Bedding Site: hidden, grassy or forested areas; beds down in a different spot each night

Young: one calf born tan, speckled with white spots; 1 per year; 35 lbs; young are able to stand shortly after birth; females form nursery groups to care for calves; young join herd at 16 days and continue to nurse for 60 days; develop adult color at 60 days

Predators: young by fox, lynx, bears, wolves and coyote

Tracks: heart-shaped, similar to white-tailed deer

Description: Usually found in remote wooded areas, the elk is dark brown to reddish brown with a yellowish rump patch. Males grow antlers that measure up to 5' across. Elk are most active during early morning and evening hours.

4½"

DID YOU KNOW...? The fisher is one of the few predators of the porcupine. It strikes the porcupine's face and then flips it over, exposing its vulnerable belly. In fact, in some areas of the country the fisher has been reintroduced by wildlife managers to reduce porcupine populations.

nocturnal

FISHER
Martes pennanti

Size: body 12-25" long; tail 13-15" long; males and females each weigh 5-14 lbs.

Habitat: dense forested areas and wooded swamps

Range: occurs throughout the Upper Peninsula

Food: snowshoe hare, mice, squirrels, porcupine, chipmunks, muskrat, raccoon, frogs, carrion, insects, berries and nuts

Mating: during March to April resulting in gestation of 30 days (after a delayed period of 9-10 months) until birth

Nest Site: a hollow tree, log, or rock crevice high above ground

Young: 1-5 kits born blind and hairless; 1 oz.; eyes open at 7 weeks; nurse for 10 weeks; kits are independent at 6 months

Predators: no natural predators

Tracks: cat-like, 5 toes, "C" shaped pad measuring 2-4" in length

Description: Found in a variety of forest types within remote wilderness areas, they occupy a range of 5-8 square miles. They have thick, glossy fur that is dark brown with silver ends.

2-4"

DID YOU KNOW...? The red fox can leap 15' in a single bound. The fox can run up to 30 mph and is an excellent swimmer. It stores uneaten food under brush piles, especially in winter.

nocturnal   *crepuscular*

Fox, Red
Vulpes vulpes

Size: body 20-40" long; tail 14-16" long; stands 14-16" high at shoulder; weighs 8-15 lbs.

Habitat: open fields near woodlands and fresh water

Range: across the state

Food: insects, nuts, corn, birds, frogs, turtle eggs, mice, rabbits and the remains of dead animals (carrion)

Mating: during December to March resulting in gestation of 52 days until birth of young

Dens: often found in hilly areas, in tree roots, under woodpiles and in abandoned woodchuck burrows; entrance is 8-15" across

Young: 5 to 10 kits born charcoal gray; 3-8 oz.; young nurse for 10 weeks, later both adults feed them regurgitated food; independent at 7 months

Predators: coyote and bobcat

Tracks: small dog-like tracks follow a straight line; claws show

Description: Seen in rural and suburban areas, the red fox shows several color variations from rusty red to black, silver and dark brown, all with white undersides. It has black legs and a white-tipped tail. It is most active at night, late morning and early evening.

2¼"

summer

winter

DID YOU KNOW...? Named for its very large feet, the snow-shoe hare is well-suited for travel on snow. It is very fast, able to reach speeds of up to 30 mph, and it can leap up to 12' in a single bound.

crepuscular

HARE, SNOWSHOE
Lepus americanus

Size: body 17-20" long; tail 2" long; weighs 4-4¼ lbs.

Habitat: dense cover of thickets, evergreen forests, wooded areas and swamps

Range: Upper Peninsula and northern parts of Lower Peninsula

Food: in spring and summer, grass, clover, dandelion, ferns; in fall and winter, bark and twigs of birch, willow, aspen trees, evergreen needles; eats own scat for added nutritional value

Mating: during February to July resulting in gestation of 36 days until birth of young

Nest Site: forms which are depressions on the ground measuring 4-6" wide and 6-8" long

Young: 2-4 young born fully mobile, covered with fur, and able to see; 2 oz. each; 2-3 litters per year; young nurse for 4 weeks at which time they are fully independent

Predators: coyotes, wolves, bobcats, foxes, martens and mink

Tracks: triangular shape; rear tracks resemble snowshoes

Description: Usually seen in open woodlands, the hare has large white hind feet. Its coat is brown in summer and white in winter. Signs of the hare include yellow to pink urine on snow. Most active at dusk and before dawn.

5½"

DID YOU KNOW...? In spite of its small size, the mink is an aggressive predator. It commonly kills prey in their burrows. The mink may dig its own den, but it often takes over abandoned woodchuck and muskrat burrows and beaver lodges.

nocturnal

MINK
Mustela vison

Size: body 11-20" long; tail 5-9" long; weighs ½ to 3½ lbs.

Habitat: marshes, rivers, lakes and streams

Range: occurs across the state

Food: fish, frogs, mice, ducks, eggs, insects, snakes, crayfish, chipmunks, rabbits, muskrat and the remains of dead animals (carrion)

Mating: during January to March resutling in gestation of 28–32 days until birth (after a delayed period of 12-43 days after mating)

Dens: lined with fur and grass; usually near waterways, often under tree roots or in abandoned burrows of woodchuck, muskrat or beaver

Young: 2-10 kits born blind and covered with fine white fur; 1-2" long weighing 1 oz.; eyes open at 25 days; nurse for 5 weeks; fully independent at 8 weeks

Predators: owls, coyote, bobcats and wolves

Tracks: show 4 of 5 toes; often seen along water's edge

Description: A sleek animal found in rural and suburban areas, the mink has glossy rich brown or black fur, with a white chin patch and occasional white spots on the belly. It has small rounded ears and is mostly active at night. Seldom stays in den for long periods.

1¾"

DID YOU KNOW...? A moose can store over 100 lbs. of food in its stomach. It has weak eyesight and has been known to mistake cars for potential mates. It can run 35 mph and can easily swim 10 miles.

crepuscular

MOOSE
Alces alces

Size: body 7½-10' long; tail 7"; stands 5-6½' at shoulder; weighs 800-1,800 lbs.

Habitat: dense, soggy wooded areas with large bogs, swamps or open water

Range: northern parts of the Upper Peninsula

Food: aspen, maple and cherry trees and water lilies

Mating: during September to November resulting in gestation of 8 months until birth of young; males make "wallows," patches of muddy ground where they urinate to attract females

Bedding Site: brushy areas of trampled vegetation; beds down in a different spot each night

Young: 1 or 2 calves born reddish brown; 25-33 lbs. each; nurse for several months; independent at 1 year

Predators: bears, wolves and to a lesser degree cougars, coyotes and wolverines prey on young

Tracks: heart-shaped with split hoof

Description: The world's largest deer, the moose is dark brown to black with a shoulder hump and a flap of skin that hangs below the throat. Males grow flattened antlers under a layer of "velvet" skin which peels away. The rack can be more than 5' across and is shed each winter.

6½"

DID YOU KNOW...? The muskrat creates a "V" shaped wave as it swims. It can hold its breath underwater for up to 15 minutes. This skill is important as the muskrat works with cattails, grass and mud to build lodges in the water. The lodges measure up to 6' high and 8' across and a good lodge can be used by several generations for 20 or 30 years.

crepuscular

MUSKRAT
Ondatra zibethicus

Size: body 9-13" long; tail 7-12" long; weighs 2-4 lbs.

Habitat: shallow wetlands that do not entirely freeze, including marshes, ponds, rivers, streams and lakes with thick vegetation

Range: across the state in rural and suburban areas

Food: water lilies, cattails, fish, frogs, crayfish, snails, apples, carrots, soybeans and clover

Mating: during February to September resulting in gestation of 25–30 days until birth

Dens: underground along the water's edge, or lodges built on platforms

Young: young born blind; weigh ¾ of an ounce; 1-11 young per litter; 2-3 litters per year; eyes open at 14-18 days; nurse for 3-4 weeks; independent at 4 weeks

Predators: red-tailed hawks, minks, great horned owls, bald eagles, foxes, coyotes and raccoons

Tracks: although they have 5 toes on each foot, only 4 show clear imprint; hind feet partly webbed

Description: The muskrat is a dark reddish brown to black rodent with slightly lighter undersides and a long, rat-like, nearly hairless tail; most active at dawn and dusk. In winter, muskrats gnaw a hole in the ice and push vegetation up through it. These are called "pushups" and are used as feeding sites.

1¼"

2"

DID YOU KNOW...? When cornered, an opossum will fall into a death-like state, (therefore the term "playing possum") for up to 3 hours. It is the only marsupial (pouched) animal native to North America, and it has 50 teeth, more than any other land mammal on this continent. It uses its prehensile (grasping) tail to hang from tree branches.

crepuscular

OPOSSUM, VIRGINIA
Didelphis virginiana

Size: body 13-20" long; tail 9-15" long; weighs 4-15 lbs.

Habitat: wooded areas and farmland near water

Range: common in southern third of Lower Peninsula and in increasing abundance northward

Food: worms, reptiles, insects, eggs, grain, garbage and remains of dead animals (carrion)

Mating: during January to May resulting in gestation of 2 weeks until birth of young

Nest Site: none; immediately after birth, young crawl into mother's kangaroo-like pouch and each attaches to one of 13 nipples

Young: 6-20 kits are born blind and hairless without well-developed rear limbs; ½" long; less than 1 oz.; 2 litters per year; nurse inside the pouch for 8 weeks, then ride on the mother's back for 4 weeks and fully independent at 12 weeks

Predators: dogs, bobcats, coyotes, foxes, hawks and owls

Tracks: hand-like tracks show "thumb" on hind foot; tail drags between feet

Description: The opossum is a grayish white, rat-like animal with hairless ears and tail, and a white face with a long, pink-nosed snout. Most active just after sunset and before dawn. Less active in winter, it rests in abandoned burrows and hollow trees.

1¾"

DID YOU KNOW...? The otter's torpedo-shaped body allows it to glide effortlessly through the water. It is accomplished at the backstroke and able to dive to depths of 50'. However, it's unable to hold its breath for more than 6-8 minutes at a time so it may be seen surfacing regularly. The otter uses "slides" or shoreline chutes into the water, and otter "rolls," which are bowl-shaped areas 20-100' from the water where they dry off and mark their territory.

crepuscular

OTTER, NORTHERN RIVER
Lontra canadensis

Size: body 18-32" long; tail 11-20" long; weighs 10-30 lbs.

Habitat: lakes, rivers and streams

Range: across state

Food: carp, sunfish, perch, trout, bass, minnows, frogs, mussels, snakes, crayfish and turtles

Mating: during December to April resulting in gestation of 60-63 days until birth of young (after a delayed period of 9-10 months after mating)

Den: located near water and lined with plant material; may use upturned logs, upturned stumps, muskrat or beaver lodges

Young: 1-5 pups born blind and fur covered; 5 oz. each; eyes open at 1 month; young explore outside the den at 2 months; continue to nurse for 4 months; fully independent at 6 months

Predators: wolves and coyotes

Tracks: often hidden by dragging tail; front and hind feet have 5 toes

Description: The otter is long and sleek with a muscular tail and a dark brown coat. Well-adapted to life in and under the water, it has a layer of fat, dense fur, webbed feet and ear and nose flaps.

3"

DID YOU KNOW...? Approximately 30,000 quills provide the porcupine with a unique defense. When confronted by a would-be attacker, it swats the animal (or person) with its tail, which is loaded with needle-sharp 4" quills. It does not shoot its quills. Hooked ends cause the quills to work their way deeper into the attacker's muscles, making them difficult to extract.

nocturnal

PORCUPINE, NORTH AMERICAN
Erethizon dorsatum

Size: body 18-23" long; tail 6-12" long; 10-28 lbs.

Habitat: forested areas

Range: in the Upper Peninsula and northern parts of Lower Peninsula

Food: clover, grass, seeds, corn, leaves and evergreen needles, aquatic plants, acorns, bark and twigs

Mating: during September to December resulting in gestation of 200-217 days until birth of young

Dens: located in hollow logs, tree cavities, under stumps and buildings, in caves and in the abandoned burrows of other animals

Young: a single pup born with dark fur and soft 1" quills; 1 lb.; pup nurses for 3 months; fully independent at 5 months

Predators: bobcats, wolverines, cougars, fishers and martens

Tracks: show long nails and bumpy pads; often hidden by dragging tail

Description: Found in remote mixed forests, the porcupine is a large, round-bodied rodent. It has color variations that include blonde, dark gray, dark brown and black, with thousands of cactus-like quills. They are most active at night, spending the day resting in trees.

2⅝"

3⅜"

DID YOU KNOW...? The raccoon is an excellent climber and swimmer. Contrary to popular belief, it does not wash everything it eats. Clever and agile, the raccoon is highly adapted to gathering and eating a great variety of foods. In the fall, it develops a thick layer of fat.

(nocturnal   Zzz deep sleeper

RACCOON, NORTHERN
Procyon lotor

Size: body 16-28" long; tail 8-12" long; stands 12" high at the shoulder; weighs 15-40 lbs.

Habitat: wooded areas near open fields, riverbanks and ponds

Range: throughout state in rural and suburban areas

Food: nuts, berries, insects, crayfish, garden vegetables, grain, rodents, remains of dead animals (carrion) and garbage

Mating: during December to January resutling in gestation of 63 days until birth of young

Dens: found in hollow trees, woodchuck burrows, culverts and under buildings

Young: 2-7 young born blind, with a light fur covering, a faint mask, and ringed tail; 4" long; 2 oz. each; eyes open at 21 days; nurse for several weeks; leave den at 10 weeks; fully independent at 4-6 months

Predators: coyotes, foxes and bobcats

Tracks: small, hand-like prints

Description: The raccoon has heavy fur streaked brown, black and gray with a distinctive black face mask and a bushy ringed tail. They are most active after dark, when they are commonly seen raiding garbage cans and getting into other mischief. They often spend the daytime sunbathing in trees.

3"

DID YOU KNOW...? The skunk is famous for defending itself with a foul-smelling spray it squirts up to 15'. Even a 3-week-old kit can spray! Usually, it first hisses, stomps its front feet and waves its tail in warning before spraying.

nocturnal **Zzz** *deep sleeper*

SKUNK, STRIPED
Mephitis mephitis

Size: body 15" long; tail 7-8"; weighs 3-10 lbs.

Habitat: wooded rural and suburban areas

Range: throughout state

Food: mice, insects, fruit, eggs and garbage

Mating: during February to March resulting in gestation of 62-66 days until birth of young

Nest Site: grass and leaf-lined dens under wood piles, in culverts and under buildings

Young: 5-7 kits born blind, wrinkled and toothless; 7 oz; eyes open at 3 weeks; (one litter per year; weaned at 8 weeks and independent at 10 weeks

Predators: few; Great Horned Owls and bobcats have been known to attack

Tracks: shows five toes across each foot

Description: The striped skunk has a glossy black coat with a thin white stripe between the eyes and a broad white "V" shape stripe on its back and down its bushy tail.

1"

DID YOU KNOW...? An Eastern gray squirrel can hide 25 nuts in half an hour. It usually finds four out of five of the nuts it buries. Nuts are also stored in tree cavities. The squirrel later finds hidden nuts by smell and it can smell a nut buried beneath 12" of snow. Its large bushy tail helps it to maintain balance while jumping from branch to branch.

diurnal

SQUIRREL, EASTERN GRAY
Sciurus carolinensis

Size: body 8-11" long; tail 8-11" long; weighs 1½ lbs.

Habitat: wooded areas

Range: throughout state

Food: nuts, seeds (including pinecones), fruits, insects, bird eggs, buds and tree bark; stores surplus food 3-4" underground

Mating: twice a year during December to February, and June to July resulting in gestation of 45 days until birth of young

Nest Site: a late winter or spring litter is often born in a tree hollow; a summer litter is born in a tree top den, a 12-19" ball-shaped nest made of leaves, twigs and bark

Young: 2-3 young born blind and hairless; weigh ½ an ounce; eyes open at 4-5 weeks; nurse for 8 weeks; independent at 12 weeks

Predators: bears, bobcats, coyotes, wolves and hawks

Tracks: front print shows 4 toes; hind shows 5

Description: Commonly seen in city parks, suburbs and wooded rural areas, this squirrel is mostly gray with a white underside and a big bushy tail. It is active all day.

2"

summer

winter

DID YOU KNOW...? The long-tailed weasel must eat two-thirds of its body weight each day. A ferocious predator, it attacks prey up to five times its size and is a threat to domestic poultry. The tip of its tail remains black to distract its own predators.

 nocturnal ● diurnal

WEASEL, LONG-TAILED
Mustela frenata

Size: body 8-10" long; tail 3-6" long; weighs 7-12 oz.

Habitat: swamps, farmland, open wooded areas and prairies near water

Range: throughout state

Food: frogs, waterfowl, rabbits, mice, muskrats, and squirrels; stores uneaten food

Mating: during June to August resulting in gestation of 25-35 days (after an 8-month delay period after mating) until birth of young

Den: lined with fur and grass; found in rock piles, hollow logs or abandoned burrows

Young: 3-9 young born blind and hairless; ⅒ oz.; eyes open at 35 days; young nurse for 3½ weeks; fully independent at 3-4 months

Predators: large hawks, owls, foxes, wild and domestic cats

Tracks: often seen in a cluster due to running and leaping, rather than in a straight line; heavily furred with 4 toes

Description: Found in remote, rural and suburban areas, the long-tailed weasel is a long, slender animal that is usually dark brown in summer and white in winter with a black-tipped tail. It is most active at night, but may be seen during the day.

1¾"

DID YOU KNOW...? The gray wolf is known as the timber wolf. A long-distance runner, it can travel 40 miles without resting, and in short bursts it can run at speeds of more than 40 mph. Its sense of smell is 100 times better than ours, and it can hear sounds from six miles away. The pack may travel up to 100 miles for a single hunt. Although usually diurnal (active during the day), they are sometimes active at night.

diurnal

WOLF, GRAY
Canis lupus

Size: body 40-52" long; tail 13-19" long; stands 26-32" high at shoulder; weighs 60-130 lbs.

Habitat: northern forests

Range: Upper Peninsula

Food: deer, moose, elk, birds, rabbits and other small mammals; pack members work together stalking and killing prey

Mating: during January to February resulting in gestation of 63 days until birth of young

Dens: usually dug by pregnant female; found in hollow logs, rocky outcroppings, or in hill-side burrows; used for 8-10 weeks

Young: 4-6 pups born blind with a dark coat; 1 lb. each; eyes open at 2 weeks; pups nurse for 6-8 weeks; fed regurgitated meat and cared for by pack members; begin to hunt with pack at 6 months; fully grown at 1 year

Predators: none

Tracks: similar to large dog with 4 toes and 1 rear pad

Description: Usually found in rural areas with plenty of undeveloped land the wolf has a mostly gray coat, but sometimes black, brown, reddish or white, with a long, bushy, black-tipped tail. Wolves live and hunt in packs of 6-12 members and they are active during the day.

4⅝"

DID YOU KNOW...? A woodchuck can dig a tunnel 5' long in one day. Their burrows often contain a network of tunnels up to 40' long. An active burrow usually has fresh dirt in front of it and has many entrances. Woodchucks begin hibernating as early as September and remain in the burrow for up to six months. The woodchuck is also known as the groundhog and despite having a day named for it, it can't really predict when winter will end.

crepuscular Zzz *hibernator*

WOODCHUCK
Marmota monax

Size: body 12-23" long; tail 4-10" long; weighs 4-14 lbs.

Habitat: pastures, meadows and brushy hillsides

Range: throughout state

Food: alfalfa, fruit, clover, daisies, dandelions, shrubs and garden vegetables

Mating: during February to April resulting in gestation of 28-30 days until birth of young

Nest Site: grass-lined burrows, located 4½' under ground

Young: 2-6 young cubs born blind and hairless; 4" long and weigh 1 ounce; young nurse for 4 weeks and are fully independent at 3 months

Predators: domestic dogs, foxes and coyotes

Tracks: show four toes on the front and five on the hind feet; multiple pads

Description: The woodchuck is a large ground mammal with coarse yellow brown to black fur, short legs and ears, a blunt nose and bushy tail.

2"

female

male

DID YOU KNOW...? The male and female Red-winged Blackbirds do not migrate together. The males return to the breeding area several weeks before the females, usually while snow is still on the ground. The male establishes and defends a nesting site to attract one or more females.

BLACKBIRD, RED-WINGED
Agelaius phoeniceus

Size: body 7½-9½" long; 10" wingspan

Habitat: wetlands and grasslands

Range: throughout state

Food: seeds and insects

Mating: early spring

Nest: bowl-shaped; attached to marsh reeds about 12" above water; cattails provide protection from weather and predators

Eggs: average clutch 3-5; pale blue marked with purple and black spots and streaks; 2-3 broods per year

Young: hatch in 11 days; females tend the eggs; males defend the nest; young hatch blind and featherless; eyes open at 1 week; flight feathers develop at 10 days; young leave nesting area at 20 days

Predators: Loggerhead Shrike, Sharp-shinned Hawk, Merlin, Great Horned Owl

Migration: migrator to southern states, Central America

Description: Found in rural, suburban and urban wetland areas, the males are black with a bright red and gold wing patch and the females are streaked black-and-white. During migration, they often flock with other species of blackbirds, such as grackles and cowbirds.

B

I

R

D

S

DID YOU KNOW...? The Northern Cardinal is very territorial. It has been known to attack its reflection in windows. It's named after the red-robed Cardinals of the Roman Catholic Church. Seven states have identified the Cardinal as their state bird, more than any other bird.

CARDINAL, NORTHERN
Cardinalis cardinalis

Size: body 7-9" long

Habitat: wooded areas

Range: permanent resident in the Lower Peninsula and the extreme southern Upper Peninsula

Food: insects, seeds, fruit and berries

Mating: April to August; during courtship males can be seen feeding females, especially at feeders

Nest: often found in pine trees; constructed of twigs and lined with grass

Eggs: average clutch 3-4; pale blue spotted with brown; 3-4 broods per year

Young: hatch in 12-13 days; young hatch blind and featherless; eyes open at 1 week; flight feathers develop at 10 days; males help care for young; young leave nesting area at 20 days

Predators: Loggerhead Shrike, Cooper's Hawk, Sharp-shinned Hawk, Merlin, Great Horned Owl

Migration: non-migrator

Description: Found in rural, suburban and urban wooded areas; the male cardinals are bright red with a prominent crest and a black face. The females are brownish yellow with a hint of red; both have a large, reddish orange, cone-shaped bill.

B
I
R
D
S

DID YOU KNOW...? The American Coot is commonly referred to as the "mudhen." It feeds throughout the day, diving for aquatic plants and skimming the surface for insects. It avoids predators by "running" across the water. They produce many young.

COOT, AMERICAN
Fulica americana

Size: body 13-17" long; weighs 1-1½ lbs.

Habitat: wetlands

Range: common migrant on large lakes and uncommon summer breeder in the Lower Peninsula and southern Upper Peninsula

Food: aquatic plants, grass, insects, small fish and tadpoles

Mating: April to May

Nest: cup-shaped; nests float hidden among cattails

Eggs: average clutch 8-12; buff with black spots

Young: hatch in 21-22 days; young have reddish orange down; males and females care for young; young leave nest 1-2 days after hatching but remain with adults for 7 weeks

Predators: Bald Eagle

Migration: migrator to southern states, Central America

Description: Often seen in rural and suburban wetlands in large flocks, this dark gray water bird has a black head and white bill with a red ring near the tip. It also has prominent red eyes and a red patch near the bill between the eyes. Its feet are lobed and olive green. It has short wings and tail. Its 3-toed lobed feet create distinct tracks along the shoreline.

B
I
R
D
S

DID YOU KNOW...? The Rock Dove, commonly called pigeon, originally came from Europe and Asia. It has a unique "homing" ability and has been used to carry messages for many years, especially during wartime. Capable of sustained flight for hundreds of miles, it can reach speeds of more than 80 mph.

DOVE, ROCK OR PIGEON
Columba livia

Size: body 11-14" long

Habitat: open wooded areas, parks, cliffs, bridges and ledges of buildingss

Range: throughout state

Food: seeds and buds

Mating: year round

Nest: often located under bridges and on barns and cliffsides; nests often lined with garbage; birds nest and roost in large flocks

Eggs: average clutch 2; white; males tend eggs during the day; females tend eggs at night; 2-3 broods per year

Young: hatch at 18 days blind and featherless; eyes open at 1 week; flight feathers develop at 10 days; young leave nesting site at 35 days

Predators: Peregrine Falcon, Great Horned Owl

Migration: non-migrator

Description: Found in rural, suburban and urban areas the Rock Dove is seen in a great variety of color patterns including blue gray, black and rust. It has an iridescent neck patch and white rump and black-banded square tail. It also has short red legs.

B
I
R
D
S

DID YOU KNOW...? Unique to North America, the Bald Eagle was chosen as our nation's symbol in 1782, narrowly beating out the Wild Turkey. It was placed on the endangered species list in 1972 due to agricultural pesticide contamination. Since the pesticide DDT was banned, the Bald Eagle population has fully recovered and it is no longer considered to be an endangered species.

EAGLE, BALD
Haliaeetus leucocephalus

Size: body 3-3½' long; 6½-8' wingspan; 8-14 lbs.

Habitat: forested areas near rivers and lakes

Range: migrates and breeds throughout the state; primary breeding is in the Upper Peninsula; some winter along major rivers and open water

Food: fish make up 90% of diet; regurgitates pellets of non-digestible parts of prey

Mating: during March to July; mated pairs return to the same nest site each spring

Nest: located in tall trees or on cliff sides

Eggs: average clutch 1-3; large, dull-white; 1 brood per year; male and female care for eggs

Young: eaglets hatch in 35 days covered with gray down; 4 oz. each; male and female care for young; by 10-12 weeks grow brown feathers flecked with white; develop adult coloration, including white head, at 4-5 years

Predators: none

Migration: migrator to southeastern states

Description: The Bald Eagle is a large, dark brown bird with white head and tail. Its eyes and beak are bright yellow.

B
I
R
D
S

DID YOU KNOW...? A strong bird of prey, the Peregrine Falcon swoops down on its prey at speeds of more than 200 mph. "Peregrine" comes from the word "peregrinate" which means to travel or wander. This falcon was placed on the Federal endangered species list in 1984 due to agricultural pesticide contamination and removed from the list in 1999. Banning the pesticide DDT has helped, and captive breeding programs have been successful.

FALCON, PEREGRINE
Falco peregrinus

Size: body 16-20" long; 40-45" wingspan; 19-40 oz.

Habitat: cliffs, bluffs and buildings

Range: found chiefly in larger cities

Food: birds, insects; it regurgitates pellets containing the non-digestible parts of their prey, including bones, feathers and hair

Mating: during April to July

Nest: often constructed on cliffs, smoke stacks and skyscrapers

Eggs: average clutch 2-5; creamy white speckled with brown

Young: hatch in 28-29 days; young covered with white down; male and female care for young, feeding them mice and birds; young develop feathers at 3 weeks and leave the nest at 6-9 weeks

Predators: none

Migration: migrates to southern states, but some remain

Description: Usually found near water, the Peregrine is brownish gray to slate blue with a dark face mask and lighter undersides that are streaked with black or brown.

DID YOU KNOW...? The Canada Goose is nicknamed "honker," because of the distinct honking sound it makes. Not all honkers migrate, but some travel from winter resting and feeding grounds in the south to summer nesting grounds in the north. They migrate in "V" shaped flocks, sometimes flying as far as 4,000 miles.

GOOSE, CANADA
Branta canadensis

Size: body 22-40" long; 5-6' wingspan; 2-18 lbs.

Habitat: lakes, ponds, marshes and rivers

Range: common summer resident throughout the state and permanent resident in the southern third of the Lower Peninsula

Food: aquatic plants, insects, grass seeds, crops

Mating during March to April; pairs mate for life

Nest: constructed on a raised site near the water's edge

Eggs: average clutch 5; large and creamy white

Young: hatch in 25-30 days; young are covered with yellowish down; males and females tend young; until they leave the nest at 45 days

Predators: larger meat-eating mammals, Great Horned Owl; goslings may be taken by snapping turtles

Migration: some migrate to southern states

Description: Found in rural, suburban and urban areas the Canada Goose is a large, light gray goose with a white chinstrap. It has a black head, neck, bill and feet. Its tracks are triangular and webbed and it moves between wetlands and farmlands or open grasslands. It is most active during the morning and afternoon.

Did You Know...? The Ruffed Grouse gets its name from the "ruff" of dark feathers on each side of its neck. Its wings are short and wide for rapid bursts of flight and can reach speeds of 40 mph. It has special comb-like membranes on its feet, allowing it to walk easily across the snow. On bitter cold days, it may burrow into the snow, which provides insulated shelter like an igloo.

GROUSE, RUFFED
Bonasa umbellus

Size: body 16-19" long; 22-25" wingspan; 1½ lbs.

Habitat: dense woodlands with open areas

Range: permanant resident throughout the state

Food: in summer ferns, mushrooms, seeds, berries and frogs; in winter, aspen and willow buds, sumac, thorn apple; young feed on insects

Mating: during April to June; as part of the mating process males stand on a log and "drum" the air by flapping their wings vigorously, creating a "thump, thump, thump" sound that can be heard up to one-half mile away

Nest: hens build nest on ground, often at base of trees

Eggs: average clutch 9-12; creamy white

Young: hatch in 24 days covered with feathers and able to feed themselves; young are able to fly short distances at 12 days; they stay with female for 3-4 months

Predators: fox, wolf, coyote, Cooper's Hawk, Northern Goshawk, Snowy Owl and Great Horned Owl

Migration: non-migrator

Description: Found in remote wilderness and rural areas, the Grouse is a gray chicken-like bird with flecks of black, white and brown and has a square, fan-shaped tail. It also has crown-like tufts of feathers on its head.

soaring

DID YOU KNOW...? The Cooper's Hawk is known as a "chicken hawk" because of its history of preying on domestic poultry. The population declined from the 1930s to the 1970s due to pesticide contamination. Its numbers have increased in recent years because of stricter pesticide regulations.

HAWK, COOPER'S
Accipiter cooperii

Size: body 14-20" long; 29-37" wingspan; 10-20 oz.; females are ⅓ larger than males

Habitat: open wooded areas

Range: nests throughout the state and permanent resident in the southern third

Food: birds, squirrels, chipmunks and other small mammals; regurgitates pellets of non-digestible parts of prey

Mating: March to July

Nest: usually found in the crotch of a tree 20-50' above the ground; constructed of sticks and lined with shredded bark; adults often return to same nest site each year

Eggs: average clutch 2-5; greenish with brown markings

Young: hatch in 36 days blind and featherless; eyes open at 1 week; flight feathers develop at 13-20 days; female tends eggs but males help care for young until they leave the nest at 30 days

Predators: none

Migration: non-migrator

Description: The Cooper's Hawk is grayish blue with white undersides and reddish bars. It has a black-capped head and three black tail stripes.

B
I
R
D
S

DID YOU KNOW...? The Red-tail is a powerful raptor (bird of prey). It has eyesight many times greater than humans and can see a small mouse or rat from hundreds of feet in the air. Listen for its high-pitched screams as it circles above its prey, then dives down to snatch it with its sharp talons. The hawk has a sharp, curved beak adapted for tearing its prey into pieces as it eats.

HAWK, RED-TAILED
Buteo jamaicensis

Size: body 19-26" long; 4-4½' wingspan; males 1½-2 lbs.; females 2-4 lbs.

Habitat: swamps, woodlands and prairies

Range: permanent resident in the southern half of the Lower Peninsula and throughout the state in the summer

Food: mice, rabbits, snakes, birds and insects; regurgitates pellets of non-digestible parts of prey

Mating: during February to June

Nest: 28-38" across; lined with shredded bark and pine needles; hawk returns to same nest site each year

Eggs: average clutch 1-4; bluish and speckled

Young: hatch in 28-32 days; young are covered with white down; males and females tend young; young leave the nest at 6-7 weeks

Predators: none; harrassed by crows

Migration: migrator to southern states

Description:. Found in rural and suburban areas, the Red-tail appears in a variety of colors from buff to brown to black-and-white, with a patterned, streaked underside. It has a bright reddish tail and is often seen perched on freeway light poles.

DID YOU KNOW...? The Great Blue Heron is the largest and most common heron species. Some young from each brood are lost. Some fall from the nest while attempting to stretch their wings and others are pushed out by larger, more aggressive chicks. This may seem tragic, but such losses are part of nature's balancing act.

HERON, GREAT BLUE
Ardea herodias

Size: body 39-52" long; 6-7' wingspan; 6-12 lbs.

Habitat: shallow lakes, ponds, rivers and marshes

Range: throughout the state in summer

Food: mice, frogs, snails, fish, insects and small birds

Mating: during April to July

Nest: 2-3' across; grouped in large colonies in tall trees along water's edge, nests are built of sticks and often are located over 100' above the ground; nests are used year after year

Eggs: average clutch 3-7; pale blue green eggs

Young: hatch featherless in 26-29 days; male and female care for young by regurgitating food into their mouths; young leave nest at 2-4 weeks

Predators: Great Horned Owl

Migration: migrator to southern states, Central and South America

Description: Found in rural and suburban wetland areas, the Great Blue Heron has a blue gray back with lighter undersides. It has a white head with a black crest, long neck, long stick-like dark legs, and a long dagger-like pale-yellow bill. Often seen standing still along the water's edge, hunting for food.

B
I
R
D
S

female

male

DID YOU KNOW...? The Ruby-throated Hummingbird flies at speeds of more than 60 mph. It can even fly backwards. Its name comes from the humming sound created by the rapid beating of its tiny wings that move at 50 –75 beats per second. It migrates to Central America each winter, flying up to 500 miles without resting.

HUMMINGBIRD, RUBY-THROATED
Archilochus colubris

Size: body 3¾" long; ⅒ oz. (about weight of a penny)

Habitat: open wooded areas

Range: throughout the state in summer

Food: flower nectar, tree sap and spiders

Mating: May to August

Nest: cup-shaped; about the size of a walnut shell; built from plant material and spider silk; located 10-20' above ground

Eggs: average clutch 2; white; pea-sized; 1-2 broods per year

Young: hatch in 16 days; feathers develop at 3-4 days; young leave the nest at 30-34 days

Predators: Loggerhead Shrike, Cooper's Hawk, Sharp-shinned Hawk and Merlin

Migration: migrator to southern states, Central and South America

Description: Hummingbirds are tiny emerald green birds found in rural and suburban areas. They have light undersides; males have a bright red throat patch and females have a white throat patch. They are attracted to bright flowers and can be seen hovering from flower to flower, sipping nectar with their long, thin bill.

B I R D S

DID YOU KNOW...? A member of the crow family, the Blue Jay is very aggressive. It often scares other birds away from feeders. Its loud cry serves as an alarm for many species of wildlife. A very bold bird, it commonly taunts and mobs birds of prey, including hawks and owls. However, it has been known to care for elderly Blue Jays.

JAY, BLUE
Cyanocitta cristata

Size: body 11-12" long; 16" wingspan; 3 oz.

Habitat: open wooded areas

Range: permanent resident throughout the state

Food: acorns, insects, fruit, seeds and the remains of dead animals (carrion); raids the nests of other birds and eats their young; stores seeds and acorns that are seldom retrieved

Mating: early spring

Nest: bulky nests in pine trees, constructed of twigs and lined with grass

Eggs: average clutch 3-6; olive-green spotted with brown; 2 broods per year

Young: hatch in 16-18 days; young hatch blind and featherless; eyes open at 1 week; flight feathers develop at 13-20 days; leave nest at 17-23 days

Predators: Cooper's Hawk, Sharp-shinned Hawk, Merlin

Migration: non-migrator

Description: Found in rural and suburban areas containing oak trees, the Blue Jay is a bright blue bird with a black necklace and white barred wings. It has a grayish white face and underside with a long wedge-shaped tail, and a distinct crest on its head.

B
I
R
D
S

female

male

DID YOU KNOW...? Often referred to as the "sparrow hawk," the American Kestrel is the smallest falcon in North America. It has "false eyes" which are actually dark spots on the back of its neck that help frighten predators. It can fly at speeds of 39 mph and hovers in place while hunting. Its keen eyesight allows it to see a grasshopper 100' away.

KESTREL, AMERICAN
Falco sparverius

Size: body 8-12" long; 20-24" wingspan; 3½-5½ oz.

Habitat: forested edges of open areas and grasslands

Range: nests throughout the state, winters in southern regions

Food: insects, rodents, birds and snakes; regurgitates pellets of non-digestible parts of prey

Mating: during late spring

Nest: located in natural cavities of trees or cliffs, also in nest boxes

Eggs: average clutch 3-5; buff with reddish brown spots

Young: hatch in 29-31 days; males and females care for eggs; young hatch blind and featherless; eyes open at 1 week; young reach adult weight at 2½ weeks; leave nest at 4 weeks

Predators: Great Horned Owl

Migration: migrator to southern states, Central America

Description: Found in rural, suburban and urban areas, the Kestrel is often seen perching on wires, fence posts, dead branches and utility poles near open spaces. It's a small falcon with a rust colored back and tail, and white chest, cheek and chin patches. Males have gray-blue wings while females have reddish brown wings.

B
I
R
D
S

DID YOU KNOW...? The bones of most bird species are hollow and lightweight, which aids them in flight. In contrast, the loon has solid bones, which helps it to dive to depths up to 150' in search of food. The adults often carry the young on their backs during the first few weeks.

LOON, COMMON
Gavia immer

Size: body 28-36" long; 49-58" wingspan; 8-12 lbs.

Habitat: large, deep lakes usually with islands and bays

Range: Upper Peninsula and parts of Lower Peninsula

Food: fish, crayfish and insects

Mating: during June to September

Nest: 2' across; commonly found on protected shoreline

Eggs: average clutch of 2 olive green eggs speckled with brown

Young: hatch in 29 days; young are covered with dark, fuzzy down; male and female care for eggs and young; independent at 2-3 months

Predators: Bald Eagle

Migration: migrator to southern states, Mexico

Description: Usually found in remote areas, the Common Loon has a black and white checkered back, a dark greenish black head, and a long, pointed black bill. It occupies a range of 10-200 acres and spends most of its time in the water searching for food.

B
I
R
D
S

DID YOU KNOW...? The Barred Owl's right ear is higher than its left ear. This helps the owl to pinpoint the location of its prey by sound alone. The Barred Owl is a favorite prey of the Great Horned Owl.

OWL, BARRED
Strix varia

Size: body 17-24" long; 40-50" wingspan; 12-23 oz.

Habitat: dense wooded areas and swamps

Range: throughout the state

Food: mice, squirrels, rabbits, birds, frogs, fish and crayfish; it regurgitates pellets containing the non-digestible parts of its prey, including bones, feathers and hair

Mating: during February to April

Nest: found in tree hollows, in abandoned nest sites of other animals, and in nest boxes

Eggs: average clutch 2-4; white

Young: hatch in 28-33 days; young hatch blind and are covered with fine white down; eyes open at 1 week; flight feathers develop at 6-9 weeks; young leave nest at 12-16 weeks

Predators: Great Horned Owl; harrassed by crows

Migration: non-migrator

Description: Found in remote wilderness, rural and suburban areas, the Barred Owl is grayish brown with dark rings around the eyes and face. It has a white and brown "barred" collar, and a brown streaked underside. It is most active at night, relying on its keen senses of hearing and sight to find prey.

B
I
R
D
S

DID YOU KNOW...? A single Great Horned Owl can eat more than 4,000 mice each year. It has the strongest talons of all owl species. The Great Horned Owl is nicknamed the "tiger with wings," because it's one of the few animals that will kill skunks and porcupines.

OWL, GREAT HORNED
Bubo virginianus

Size: body 18-25" long; up to 44" wingspan; 3-6 lbs.; females slightly larger than males

Habitat: open wooded areas

Range: throughout the state

Food: smaller owls, hawks, waterfowl and other birds, mice, skunks, reptiles and insects; regurgitates pellets of non-digestible parts of prey

Mating: during January to February

Nest: found in tree hollows, nesting boxes and in abandoned nests of squirrels, hawks and crows

Eggs: average clutch 1-5; white; male brings food to female while she tends the eggs

Young: hatch in 28-32 days blind and covered with fine down; eyes open at 7-10 days; young gain flight feathers at 6-9 weeks

Predators: none; harrassed by crows

Migration: non-migrator

Description: Found in remote wilderness, rural and suburban areas, the Great Horned Owl is a large, reddish brown to gray or black owl with lighter, streaked undersides. It has a white throat collar, horn-like tufts of feathers on its head and yellow eyes. It is most active at night, relying on its keen senses of hearing and sight to find its prey.

B
I
R
D
S

female

male

DID YOU KNOW...? The Ring-necked Pheasant will often run for cover rather than flying to avoid danger. However, it is capable of flight speeds of 45 mph for short distances. The average age of a pheasant is less than 1 year. A non-native species imported from China in 1818, the Pheasant is often seen along roadsides ingesting small pebbles, known as grit, which help to break down and digest its food.

PHEASANT, RING-NECKED
Phasianus colchicus

Size: body 22-35" long including tail; 28-30" wingspan; 2-3 lbs.

Habitat: prairies and farmland; cattail marshes for winter cover

Range: chiefly in the southern half of Lower Peninsula

Food: grass and weed seeds, crops and insects

Mating: late March-August; peak April-June

Nest: hens build nests on the ground, often in hay fields

Eggs: average clutch 12; greenish brown

Young: hatch at 23-25 days covered with feathers and able to feed themselves; young are able to fly short distances at 1 week, but they remain with the female for 10-12 weeks

Predators: fox, wolf, coyote, Snowy Owl, Great Horned Owl, Northern Goshawk, Peregrine Falcon

Migration: non-migrator

Description: Usually found in rural fields, fence rows, ditches and thickets, males are coppery brown with black necks. They have a greenish black head with a red eye patch and a white ring around the neck. Their long tapered tails may reach 15". Females are pale brown with shorter tails. They are most active during the morning and afternoon.

female

male

DID YOU KNOW...? At night the Bobwhite Quail roosts in a group called a covey. They form a circle on the ground with their bodies touching and their heads facing out. This keeps them warm and allows them to watch for predators. The covey is usually made up of 10-15 birds.

QUAIL, BOBWHITE
Colinus virginianus

Size: body 8-10" long; short tail; 13" wingspan; 7 oz.

Habitat: farmland and open wooded areas

Range: southern half of Lower Peninsula

Food: weed and pine seeds, acorns, berries, grain and insects

Mating: during March-June

Nest: males and females build ground nests in tall grass

Eggs: average clutch 12-15; buff-colored

Young: hatch in 23 days with feathers and able to feed themselves; young stay with female for up to 4 months

Predators: fox, wolf, coyote, Snowy Owl, Great Horned Owl, Northern Goshawk, Peregrine Falcon

Migration: non-migrator

Description: The Bobwhite Quail is found in rural farmlands, grasslands and open wooded areas. The males are a dark reddish brown with a white throat, a black collar and a stripe near the eyes that extends to the base of the neck. Females are similar but have a buff-colored throat and no black collar. They are most active at sunrise and in the late afternoon; often seek cover in heavy brush.

B
I
R
D
S

DID YOU KNOW...? The American Robin uses "anting" to rid itself of lice and other parasites. The bird positions itself near an anthill and allows ants to crawl all over its body. Robins are not listening for worms when they cock their heads from side to side. Because their eyes are placed far back on the sides of their heads, they must turn their heads from side to side to look at things. The American Robin is the Michigan state bird.

ROBIN, AMERICAN
Turdus migratorius

Size: body 9-11" long; 2-3 oz.

Habitat: open wooded areas and farmland

Range: throughout the state

Food: earthworms, insects, fruits and berries

Mating: early spring

Nest: females build nests out of mud, grass and twigs; found in trees, shrubs and house gutters

Eggs: average clutch 3-5; pale blue; 2 broods per year

Young: hatch in 12-14 days; young hatch blind and featherless; eyes open at 1 week; flight feathers develop at 13-20 days

Predators: Merlin, Sharp-shinned Hawk, Cooper's Hawk

Migration: migrator to southern states, Central America

Description: Early arrivals each spring, Robins are usually found poking around lawns in search of earthworms. Males have slate-gray backs, rusty red chests and white speckled throats. Females are gray brown with pale orange chests. They often form large migrating flocks in the fall.

B
I
R
D
S

DID YOU KNOW...? The Barn Swallow feeds while flying. It skims over ponds and fields to catch insects in its wide mouth. Each fall it migrates south to areas where insects are plentiful.

SWALLOW, BARN
Hirundo rustica

Size: body 5½ -7" long

Habitat: farmland, and open wooded areas often near water

Range: throughout the state

Food: airborne insects

Mating: during April to June; pairs mate for life

Nest: small, cup-like nests, made almost entirely of mud and lined with feathers; often located in small colonies on bridges, barns and sheds

Eggs: average clutch 4-5; white with reddish brown spots; 2 broods per year

Young: hatch in 13-17 days, blind and featherless; eyes open at 1 week; flight feathers develop at 13-20 days; males and females tend young; leaves nest at 18-23 days

Predators: Loggerhead Shrike, Merlin, Sharp-shinned Hawk

Migration: migrator to South America

Description: Found in rural and suburban areas, Barn Swallows are a dark, steel-blue with rusty orange undersides. They have a deeply forked tail with white markings.

DID YOU KNOW...? Wild Turkeys form flocks of 6-40 birds and roost in trees each evening. In spring, males perform elaborate courtship displays to attract females. In 1782, it lost by a single vote to the Bald Eagle as the national bird. In 1900 the Wild Turkey population was less than 100,000 due to habitat loss. Today, thanks to better wildlife management, Wild Turkey numbers have grown to nearly 4½ million.

TURKEY, WILD
Meleagris gallopavo

Size: body 3-4' long; 5' wingspan; males weigh 16-25 lbs.; females weigh 9-11 lbs.

Habitat: open wooded areas and brushy grasslands

Range: central parts of Lower Peninsula and southern parts of Upper Peninsula

Food: ferns, grass, buds, berries, insects and acorns

Mating: during April to May

Nest: hens build nest on the ground, usually a leaf-lined hollow in heavy brush

Eggs: average clutch 10-18; buff with tan markings

Young: hatch in 28 days covered with feathers and able to feed themselves; young are able to fly at 3-4 weeks, but they remain with the female for up to 4 months

Predators: wolf, Great Horned Owl

Migration: non-migrator

Description: Found in remote wilderness, rural and sub-urban areas, the Wild Turkey is a large, dark brown and black bird with fan tail. Males have wattles (fleshy growths that hang beneath the chin), spurs (bony spear-like projections on the back of each leg), a snood (a flap of skin that drapes over the bill), and a hair-like chest beard. Females are more drab. They are most active in the daytime and they are strong fliers.

B
I
R
D
S

DID YOU KNOW...? The American Woodcock is also known as the "Timberdoodle" and the "Bog Sucker." It has large eyes and incredible 360-degree (full circle) vision. Its bill has highly sensitive nerve endings that can detect the movement of earthworms beneath the soil. In spite of its short wings, the Woodcock is capable of flight speeds of 13 mph.

WOODCOCK, AMERICAN
Scolopax minor

Size: body 10-12" long; 8-10 oz.

Habitat: open wooded areas and wetlands

Range: throughout the state

Food: earthworms, grubs and insects

Mating: during March to June

Nest: ground nest; measures 4-5" across

Eggs: average clutch 4; buff-colored with brown specks

Young: hatch in 20-21 days; young hatch covered with down and able to feed themselves; young reach adult size at 25 days and are able to fly; fully independent at 6-8 weeks

Predators: fox, wolf, coyote, Short-eared Owl

Migration: migrates to southern states

Description: Found in rural and suburban wooded areas the Woodcock is a cinnamon-colored bird with dark brown blotches and extensive barring. It has short, pinkish legs, a short neck, tail and wings. It is most active at night and early in the morning; look for rectangular holes (⅛" wide) in the soil made by its probing bill.

female

male

DID YOU KNOW...? The Downy Woodpecker has a chiseled bill it uses to tunnel into tree bark and a tongue specially adapted to spear insects. It uses its tail for support as it searches for food on tree trunks or excavates a nesting cavity. Each year, it excavates a new nesting site. Old sites become weatherproof nesting sites and burrows for other birds and wildlife.

WOODPECKER, DOWNY
Picoides pubescens

Size: 5-6" long

Habitat: wooded areas

Range: throughout the state

Food: insects and insect larvae

Mating: during early springtime

Nest: deep holes in trees, 1" wide

Eggs: average clutch 4-5; white; 1 brood per year; males and females tend eggs

Young: hatch in 11-12 days; young hatch blind and featherless; eyes open at 1 week; flight feathers appear at 13-20 days; young leave nest at 20-25 days

Predators: Loggerhead Shrike, Northern Shrike, Sharp-shinned Hawk, Merlin

Migration: non-migrator

Description: Found in remote, rural and suburban areas, the Downy Woodpecker is a distinctive black and white bird with white underside and striped wings. The male has a red patch on its head. Two forward-facing toes and two rear-facing toes help this bird to move up and down tree trunks.

B
I
R
D
S

female

male

DID YOU KNOW...? The Pileated Woodpecker is the largest woodpecker in North America. With its strong neck muscles, a thick skull, and short feathers that keep sawdust out of its nostrils, it is highly adapted to drilling holes in trees. Its tongue is so long that it wraps inside around the back of the skull over its head and into the bird's right nostril. Specialized muscles work to contract and extend its tongue.

WOODPECKER, PILEATED
Dryocopus pileatus

Size: body 16-19½" long; 27-30" wingspan; 10-16 oz.

Habitat: wooded areas

Range: Upper Peninsula and northern Lower Peninsula

Food: berries, fruits, nuts, insects and insect larvae

Mating: during March to April; pairs mate for life

Nest: male and female begin construction of a nesting cavity in February rectangular or oval in shape with an 8" opening; usually located 40' above the forest floor on the south side of a tree

Eggs: average clutch 4; white

Young: hatch in 18 days blind and featherless; eyes open at 1 week; flight feathers develop at 13-20 days; male and female tend young; young are independent at 6 months

Predators: none

Migration: non-migrator

Description: Found in mature woods, rural areas and parks; this is a large woodpecker with a black back, white neck and throat. It has a red crest, black chisel-like bill and long spear-like tongue. Males have a red mustache.

B
I
R
D
S

LIFELIST

Place a check by each mammal or bird you've seen whether in your backyard, on a camping trip or at the zoo.

Critters

☐ **Badger, American**

Location: _____ Date: _____

Comments: _____

☐ **Bat, Little Brown**

Location: _____ Date: _____

Comments: _____

☐ **Bear, Black**

Location: _____ Date: _____

Comments: _____

☐ **Beaver**

Location: _____ Date: _____

Comments: _____

☐ **Bobcat**

Location: _____ Date: _____

Comments: _____

☐ **Chipmunk, Eastern**

Location: _____ Date: _____

Comments: _____

☐ **Cottontail, Eastern**

Location: _____ Date: _____

Comments: _____

☐ **Coyote**

Location: _____ Date: _____

Comments: _____

☐ **Deer, White-tailed**

Location: _____ Date: _____

Comments: _____

☐ **Elk**

Location: _____ Date: _____

Comments: _____

☐ **Fisher**

Location: _____ Date: _____

Comments: _____

☐ **Fox, Red**

Location: _____ Date: _____

Comments: _____

☐ **Hare, Snowshoe**

Location: _____ Date: _____

Comments: _____

☐ **Mink**

Location: _____ Date: _____

Comments: _____

☐ **Moose**

Location: _____ Date: _____

Comments: _____

☐ **Muskrat**

Location: _____ Date: _____

Comments: _____

☐ **Opossum**

Location: _____ Date: _____

Comments: _____

☐ **Otter, Northern River**

Location: _____ Date: _____

Comments: _____

☐ **Porcupine**

Location: _____ Date: _____

Comments: _____

☐ **Raccoon**

Location: _____ Date: _____

Comments: _____

☐ **Skunk, Striped**

Location: _____ Date: _____

Comments: _____

☐ **Squirrel, Eastern Gray**

Location: _____ Date: _____

Comments: _____

☐ **Weasel, Long-tailed**

Location: _____ Date: _____

Comments: _____

☐ **Wolf, Gray**

Location: _____ Date: _____

Comments: _____

☐ **Woodchuck**

Location: _____ Date: _____

Comments: _____

Birds

☐ **Blackbird, Red-winged**

Location: _____ Date: _____

Comments: _____

☐ **Cardinal, Northern**

Location: _____ Date: _____

Comments: _____

☐ **Coot, American**

Location: _____ Date: _____

Comments: _____

☐ **Dove, Rock or Pigeon**

Location: _____ Date: _____

Comments: _____

☐ **Eagle, Bald**

Location: _____ Date: _____

Comments: _____

☐ **Falcon, Peregrine**

Location: _____ Date: _____

Comments: _____

☐ **Goose, Canada**

Location: _____ Date: _____

Comments: _____

☐ **Grouse, Ruffed**

Location: _____ Date: _____

Comments: _____

☐ **Hawk, Cooper's**

Location: _____ Date: _____

Comments: _____

☐ **Hawk, Red-tailed**

    Location: _____ Date: _____

    Comments: _____

☐ **Heron, Great Blue**

    Location: _____ Date: _____

    Comments: _____

☐ **Hummingbird, Ruby-throated**

    Location: _____ Date: _____

    Comments: _____

☐ **Jay, Blue**

    Location: _____ Date: _____

    Comments: _____

☐ **Kestrel, American**

    Location: _____ Date: _____

    Comments: _____

☐ **Loon, Common**

    Location: _____ Date: _____

    Comments: _____

☐ **Owl, Barred**

    Location: _____ Date: _____

    Comments: _____

☐ **Owl, Great Horned**

    Location: _____ Date: _____

    Comments: _____

☐ **Pheasant, Ring-necked**

    Location: _____ Date: _____

    Comments: _____

☐ **Quail, Bobwhite**

    Location: _____ Date: _____

    Comments: _____

☐ **Robin, American**

    Location: _____ Date: _____

    Comments: _____

☐ **Swallow, Barn**

    Location: _____ Date: _____

    Comments: _____

☐ **Turkey, Wild**

    Location: _____ Date: _____

    Comments: _____

☐ **Woodcock, American**

    Location: _____ Date: _____

    Comments: _____

☐ **Woodpecker, Downy**

    Location: _____ Date: _____

    Comments: _____

☐ **Woodpecker, Pileated**

    Location: _____ Date: _____

    Comments: _____

WILD WORDS

A

Adaptation: a particular characteristic developed by a plant or animal that makes it better suited to its environment.

Amphibians: cold-blooded, smooth-skinned vertebrates that spend part of their life on land and part of their life in the water including frogs, toads, newts and salamanders.

Anthropomorphism: attributing human characteristics to animals.

Antler: bony projections grown and shed each year by members of the deer family, typically males. Antlers are used in courtship rivalries between competing males.

B

Behavior: the way in which an animal responds to its environment.

Brood: (noun) the offspring of birds hatched at one time; (verb) to hatch, protect and warm the young, usually done instinctively by the female.

Browse: (noun) portions of woody plants including twigs, shoots and leaves used as food by animals such as deer; (verb) to eat parts of woody plants.

Brumation: a period of winter dormancy brought on by dropping temperatures during which a reptile's or amphibian's body processes are slowed down, and they become immobile.

Buck: a male deer, goat, pronghorn or rabbit.

Bull: a male moose, elk or bison.

Burrow: (noun) a hole, tunnel or underground den excavated by an animal for shelter or refuge; (verb) to dig underground.

C

Camouflage: a protective adaptation that enables an animal to disguise itself or blend with its surroundings.

Carnivore: an animal that eats other animals; a meat eater.

Carrion: the body of a dead animal in the natural state of decay, which serves as a food source for other animals.

Clutch: a nest of eggs.

Cold-blooded (ectothermic): an animal whose body temperature is dependent upon and varies with the temperature of its environment (e.g., fish, amphibians and reptiles).

Communication: sound, scent or behavior recognized by members of the same species and sometimes by other species.

Competition: different species of animals that use the same source for food or shelter.

Conservation: the care, wise use and management of a resource.

Consumer: an animal that gets its food from producers (plants).

Courtship: a behavior or series of actions an animal displays to indicate to the opposite sex that it is ready to mate in order to reproduce.

Cover: naturally-occurring sheltered areas that provide concealment and shelter for wildlife, such as a dead tree, fallen log, rock outcrops, dense areas of brush or trees.

Cow: a female moose, wapiti (elk) or bison.

Crepuscular: active in twilight at dawn and dusk.

D

Diurnal: active during the day.

Doe: a female deer, pronghorn or rabbit.

Down: a layer of soft, fine feathers that provides insulation.

Drake: a male duck.

E

Ecology: the study of the relationships between living things and the environments in which they live.

Ecosystem: an interacting system of plants, animals, soil and climactic conditions in a self-contained environment (e.g., pond, marsh, swamp, lake or stream).

Endangered: a species in danger of becoming extinct due to declining population numbers.

Environment: the entire surroundings of an organism (plant or animal) or group of organisms.

Estuary: area where fresh water and salt water meet.

Ethics: principles of good conduct; a sense of right and wrong.

Exotic: a foreign species introduced to an area from another region or ecosystem. Exotic species are considered undesirable as they compete with native species for habitat and food.

Extinct: a species that no longer exists or has died out.

F

Fledgling: young birds learning to fly.

Food chain: plants and animals linked together as sources and consumers of food; typically an organism higher in the food chain eats one lower in the food chain, so the health of one is dependent on the health of another.

Food web: the many possible feeding relationships found within a given ecosystem.

Forage: (noun) plant material such as grasses, ferns, shrubs and the leaves and twigs of trees; (verb) to eat plant material.

G

ame species: wildlife that can be hunted or trapped according to legal seasons and limits.

estation: length of pregnancy.

H

abitat: the local environment in which an animal lives. Components include food, water, cover (shelter) and space.

abitat enhancement: the development and improvement of habitat (including sources of food, water, cover and space) for the benefit of fish or wildlife.

en: a female pheasant, duck, quail or turkey.

erbivore: an animal that eats only plant material.

ibernation: a period of winter dormancy during which an animal's body processes slow dramatically, reducing the amount of energy required for survival. True hibernators' body processes slow nearly to a stop, and they require much less energy to survive. Deep sleepers' body processes do not slow as much, and they are more easily awakened.

ome range: the area over which an animal repeatedly travels in order to locate food, water and cover.

orn: hard protrusions that continuously grow on the head of certain mammals such as the bighorn sheep and bison. Horns are made of keratin, the same material that makes fingernails.

ncubate: to warm eggs (usually bird eggs) with body heat so they develop and hatch. Females typically incubate the eggs.

Introduced species: a plant or animal brought from another region, often another continent, either intentionally or by accident; introduced species can have positive or negative effects on the native species. Also referred to as "exotic" or "non-native," especially when the result is negative.

Invertebrates: animals without backbones, including insects, earthworms, spiders and mollusks (e.g. snails).

J-L

Land ethic: deliberate, thoughtful and responsible consideration for the natural landscape and natural resources, including wildlife, fossil fuels, soil, water and timber.

Land management: the purposeful manipulation of land or habitat by people to encourage wildlife populations to increase, decrease or stabilize in number. In the case of wildlife, this involves managing food, water, cover and space to affect population numbers.

Larva: the newly hatched, earliest stage that differs greatly from the appearance and form of the adult; usually used in relation to insects, but sometimes also for amphibians.

M

Mammal: a warm-blooded animal that has fur or hair and produces milk to feed its young.

Migration: the seasonal movements of fish and wildlife from one area to another usually triggered by length of daylight hours. Animals that move varying distances at irregular times dependent upon weather and availability of food are partial migrators. Animals that move to the same places at the same times every year are complete migrators.

N

Native: an indigenous or naturally occurring species of plant or animal.

atural resource: materials found in nature to which people have assigned value such as timber, fresh water, wildlife and fossil fuels (coal and oil).

octurnal: an animal that is active by night.

ongame species: the majority of wildlife not hunted by humans including songbirds, raptors, reptiles and amphibians.

onrenewable resources: nonliving natural resources which, for all practical purposes, cannot be replaced, including metallic minerals (e.g. gold and copper) and fossil fuels (e.g. coal and oil).

mnivore: an animal that eats both plants and animals (meat).

pportunist: an animal that can take advantage of any number of food sources available.

heromone: a chemical scent secreted as a means of communication between members of the same species.

hotosynthesis: the process by which plant cells convert light, water and carbon dioxide into energy and nutrients while simultaneously releasing oxygen.

lumage: the feathers of a bird.

ollution: toxic (poisonous) substances deposited in the air, water or soil creating an unhealthy environment.

opulation: a collection of individuals of the same species in a given area whose members can breed with one another.

redator: an animal that hunts and feeds on other animals (prey).

rey: an animal hunted or killed for food by other animals (predators).

roducers: plants that obtain energy from the sun and produce food through the process of photosynthesis.

Q-R

Range: the particular geographic region in which a species is found

Raptor: a bird of prey; includes falcons, owls, eagles, hawks, kites, vultures and ospreys.

Recreation: an activity undertaken for enjoyment; entertainment often associated with natural resources (water, forests, rock formations) includes rock climbing, bird watching, fishing, canoeing and hunting.

Renewable natural resource: a natural resource that can be replenished and harvested, including trees and wildlife.

Reptiles: cold-blooded vertebrate animals that have scales or hard plates covering their bodies (e.g., snakes, lizards and turtles).

Riparian area: lands adjacent to streams, rivers, lakes and other wetlands where the vegetation is influenced by the great availability of water.

Roost: refers to a safe gathering place used by wildlife, usually birds and bats, for rest or sleep.

Rut: activity associated with breeding behavior.

S

Scat: refers to defecation, excrement or waste.

Scavenger: an animal that feeds on the remains of dead animals

Scrape: an area where concentrated amounts of urine are mixed with mud to attract a mate or indicate territory.

Season: time of year when game species may be legally harvested

Sow: a female bear.

Species: a group of animals that have similar structure, common ancestors and characteristics they maintain through breeding.

ewardship: responsible care of natural resources for future generations.

ocking: the artificial propagation and introduction of game species into an area.

rritory: the area an animal will defend, usually during breeding season, against intruders of its own species.

reatened: a classification for wildlife species whose population is in great decline and approaching the "endangered" classification.

-V

rtebrates: animals with a backbone, including fish, birds, mammals, reptiles and amphibians.

/-Z

arm-blooded (endothermic): an animal whose body temperature is unrelated to its environment (e.g., mammals and birds).

ean: (noun) young that no longer depend on an adult for food; (verb) to withhold mother's milk from young and substitute other nourishment.

ildlife: nondomesticated plants and animals (including mammals, birds, fish, reptiles, insects and amphibians).

ildlife agency: a state or federal organization responsible for managing wildlife.

ildlife management: a combination of techniques, scientific knowledge and technical skills used to protect, conserve and manage wildlife and habitat.

inter kill: the death of animals during winter resulting from lack of food and exposure to cold.

WILDLIFE FOREVER PROJECTS IN MICHIGAN

Working at the grassroots level, Wildlife Forever (WF) ha
completed conservation projects in all 50 states.

- Raised and released 7,500,000 walleyes into Little & Big Bays de Noc
- Stabilized 500 feet of eroding bank on the Big Sable Rive
  the largest source of water to Hablin Lake, a 4,900-acre fishing lake
- Studied the roosting requirements of the endangered Indiana bat.
- Constructed a walleye-rearing pond.
- Created a containment site to hold dredged silt to improve Lowe
  Scott Lake for fish.
- Supported a winter emergency feeding program for white-tailed dee
- Printed proceedings from the 57th Midwest Fish & Wildlife Conference
- Produced interpretive materials for Jack Pine Wildlife Viewing Tour
- Improved stream habitat for trout on Bigelow Creek by installin
  eight habitat improvement structures on a 3,500-foot stretch.
- Purchased yeast, soybean meal, and fertilizer for four fish-rearin
  ponds, which provide over 1 million walleye fry for the Saginaw Ba
- Constructed two earthen dams with a control structure and place
  rip-rap to improve waterfowl habitat at the Big Gulch and Outla
  Impoundments in Huron National Forest.
- Restored two wetland basins (totaling over 300 acres) along count
  drains in Southern Lower Michigan to improve habitat for waterfo
  and other wildlife.
- Restored 89 acres of wetlands for waterfowl along Kurtz, Wallac
  and Bryant Creeks in Alcona County.
- Studied seasonal habits, population and activity of great gray owls i
  eastern Upper Peninsula.
- Supported winter feeding of 3,500 wild turkeys in Upper Peninsula

RULER

Find tracks? Use this guide to measure them.

centimeters

0 1 2 3 4 5 6 7 8 9

inches

0 1 2 3 4 5